The Little Woodcock

The Little Woodcock

By Berniece Freschet

Illustrated by Leonard Weisgard

Charles Scribner's Sons *New York*

For my nieces and nephews: Suzanne, Sandra, Scott, Stacy, Stephen, and little Sheila

The Little Woodcock

At the tangled edge of the damp March woods, hidden under an alder thicket, a little woodcock sits on her nest.

Under her warm feathers, in the nest of dry leaves, lie four tan and reddish-brown spotted eggs.

Her feathers so closely match the colors of the ground and brush and she sits so quietly that it is hard to see her.

The tiny marsh wren, dancing and twittering on a twig just above the woodcock, does not see her.

A cottontail hops close, but he does not know she is there.

A hungry fox trots near. He stops and circles around the bush. He seems to look right at the little woodcock.

She sits very still, for she knows that danger is close by. Her heart beats faster, but she does not turn her head.

She does not blink an eye.

She does not even ruffle a feather.

She is as still as the stones on the ground.

All through the woods, the brown birds—grouse, quail, and partridge—sit quietly on their nests among rocks and leaves. But no bird or animal can hide himself as well as the little woodcock.

Only if you look very closely you might see some part of her—her long pointed bill or one bright, unblinking eye.

The fox pokes his nose into the bush. He seems to know that something is there, but even his keen eyes cannot see her sitting so still. Soon he trots away. He would be angry if he knew that he had missed a supper.

When the sun sets and it is dusk, the woodcock leaves the thicket. It is time for her to go with her mate to the bog to hunt for worms.

She does not fly into the air at once but first moves further away from the nest. If an enemy lurks nearby and sees her fly up, she will not reveal the hiding place of her eggs.

There is another reason. When she takes flight, the rapid stroking of her broad wings makes a vibrant, whistling sound, and this noise alerts her enemies. Sometimes she is called "Little Whistler."

She flutters up, flying low over the tops of bush and thicket. But almost immediately she drops quickly back to the ground. She is dodging out of sight. For, besides the fox, the weasel and the lynx might be looking for their suppers.

Again she takes to the air. Her mate, who has been hiding under a bush close by, joins her now. They fly side by side.

Suddenly an explosion shatters the quiet of the evening!

Her mate falls!

In panic, the little woodcock flies swiftly.

She drops into a thick hedge. She sees the hunter come, lift her mate, and carry him away. Man is the woodcock's most dangerous enemy.

She stays hidden a long time, but finally hunger forces her to look for food. She flies to the bog, but she does not stay long this evening. She is uneasy and lifts her head often to listen to the noises of the night.

A cold wind ruffles the feathers on her back. She feels a sudden new chill in the air, and she flies quickly back to her nest.

Snow begins to fall.

As always, the woodcock and her mate were among the earliest of the spring birds to return from the warm south to the woods of the north. Because they migrate early, there is the danger of being caught in a sudden freeze or blizzard. Then many are lost.

The wind blows harder, catching the snowflakes and swirling them into a thick, white curtain that shuts out the world. All that night the snow falls and the cold wind blows.

By morning the little woodcock is completely buried under the white drifts.

She huddles there all through the day, but that evening she bursts out of her snow blanket.

She flies to the bog to look for food—and then to the brook for water.

But the snow is deep. There is no food to be found, and the watering places are frozen over. The little woodcock knows she must not be away from her nest for too long. She hurries back.

The next day the warm breezes of spring blow gently through the woods. The snow begins to melt. In another day a tiny rivulet of water trickles near. The woodcock drinks.

Later she finds several grubs and beetles by an old fallen log. This year she is lucky—she will not have to abandon her nest.

The mother bird has been sitting on her nest for three weeks now, and she knows that it is almost time for her eggs to hatch.

It is the middle of the day, and she stretches her wings and for a few moments enjoys the warmth of the April sunlight. Then, carefully, she settles herself back on the eggs.

But in a little while she stands and moves restlessly to the edge of the nest. She cocks her head and looks down at the eggs.

One of the shells has a tiny crack.

She hears light, tapping sounds.

The crack is wider now.

The egg is breaking open. In it lies a wet, scraggly baby chick!

There are more soft, tapping sounds. The other baby chicks inside the eggs are trying to break out of their shells. As all baby birds do, each chick pecks at the shell walls with the egg tooth on the top of its bill. Later the tooth will disappear.

At last all the eggs are broken.

Four new baby chicks lie in the bottom of the nest.

The warm spring air dries them. The little chicks are covered with fluffy, striped down. They are very tiny, not even as big as a man's thumb. Their bills are short, but they will grow longer as their bodies grow bigger.

Their eyes are round and dark as blackberries. They flutter their stubby wings, jostling each other as they try to move about the nest, but they are still very weak.

The mother woodcock stretches her wings and gathers her babies close. She is very proud of her handsome new family.

Before long, when the babies are stronger, the mother takes her new family for a walk. They follow behind her, moving in a single file, with their bills pointing downward.

They poke under the dead leaves and in among the skunk cabbages, looking for small insects and larvae.

"Peep—peep," they call.

Overhead, there is a sudden rustling in the beech tree.

At once the woodcock is still. She cheeps a warning. Instinctively, the little chicks become as still as their mother.

It is only the red squirrel. He runs to the end of the branch and jumps to a bough below.

It does not take long to satisfy the tiny chicks' hunger, and soon mother woodcock leads her family back to the safety of the thicket. They settle themselves comfortably in the nest for a nap.

When the sun slides behind the green hills and the shadows of twilight move softly through the woods, the little woodcock awakens. She stretches leg and wing.

This is the hour when the hermit thrush fills the air with the beautiful, flutelike music of his song.

As the day creatures snuggle down to sleep, the creatures of the night begin to stir. Not for away, sitting on a fallen log, a whippoorwill calls his name. . . .

Whip-poor-will. . .   whip-poor-will. . .   whip-poor-will. . .

From the top of a tall maple tree, five small, furry bodies hurl themselves into space. These are the flying squirrels. They leap far out, spreading their legs wide. The skin between their front and hind legs acts as a parachute as they glide from tree to tree.

Tonight the little woodcock is especially hungry, for sensing that her eggs were ready to hatch, she has hardly left her nest in the past three days.

She cheeps a warning to her chicks. Then she listens, and hearing only the familiar sounds of evening, she leaves the thicket.

The hunter and his dog know that it is time for the woodcock to be out, and they head for the woods.

Suddenly the whippoorwill stops singing in the middle of his song.

The woods become still—as though all in it are listening.

The little mother bird, warned by the silence that danger is near, scurries under a hazel bush.

The man comes quietly through the woods, the dog following at his heels. The hunter moves past the nest and stands for a moment only a step away from where the little woodcock is hiding.

Her heart beats wildly.

The dog sniffs among the dry leaves. But nature, besides giving the woodcock her feathers as a camouflage, has also given her very little odor, and so the dog must be almost upon her before he can pick up her scent.

The man and the dog walk on.

When once again the little woodcock hears the call of the whippoorwill, she knows it is safe to leave her hiding place.

She takes wing and soon alights at the edge of the marshy bog. Here she pushes her long, sensitive bill into the mud, probing for her favorite meal of earthworms.

Her eyes, set toward the back of her head, behind her ears, keep a lookout for enemies. These remarkable eyes can see movement in front and even behind her back.

From the marsh come the clear calls of the spring peepers, and the deep bass voice of a bullfrog joins the chorus.

The moon rises. A pair of raccoons amble by on their way to the brook to catch fish for their supper.

A bat swoops down. He dives and snaps at a mosquito and then flies on, looking for moths and other insects of the night.

The woodcock is a member of the snipe family, and some of her cousins are here at the bog tonight. As she searches for worms, she hears the low voices of the curlew, the plover, and the jacksnipe.

All around the busy woodcock is a circle of small holes where she has poked her bill into the soft, wet earth. The tip of her upper bill is flexible, as though it were hinged, and she easily grasps the worms that she finds in the damp ground.

In a little while she flutters up into the air. She flies back to the nest to warm her chicks.

Many times this night the whistling sound of the little woodcock's wings is heard as she flies back and forth from the bog to the nest, making sure that her babies are warm and safe.

During one visit to the bog, as she is busy digging, a sound interrupts her work.

She stops a moment to watch a fat skunk turning over rocks and pieces of wood, looking for beetles and grasshoppers.

CURLEW

PLOVER

ACKSNIPE

She pushes her bill back into the earth, but then another sound—a frightening voice from the meadow—makes her lift her head. She listens.

There it is again.

The hunting cry of the screech owl!

The woodcock must hurry to the nest. She wings swiftly back to the woods. She barely has time to gather her chicks under her and settle herself when a soft rush of air tells her that the owl is near.

She hears him fly into a big oak tree nearby. She can tell by the sound of his movements that he has gone into the hole at the top of the tree.

Soon the owl comes out and sits on a branch. He turns his head halfway around and snaps his beak hungrily. Then he flies softly away. He has gone to the meadow to look for mice.

If he returns, the little woodcock will know that the owl has decided to make his home in the old oak tree. Then this will no longer be a safe place for her chicks. She waits quietly.

The woodcock watches a possum crawl out of a hollow stump where she, too, has been hiding from the owl. The possum is gathering clean new grass. It is time to line her den and make it warm for the tiny baby possums that will soon arrive. She carries her harvest of grass away in the loop of her tail.

The woodcock does not dare to leave her nest again tonight. She sits and listens to the sounds that are all about her. She can hear the friendly chirping of the crickets and the tiny scurrying feet of the wood mice. Now and then she hears the far-off hooting of the owl.

In the east the dark sky is beginning to streak with light when the soft sound of swishing air tells the woodcock that the owl has come back.

He alights in the old oak tree. She hears him stretch his wings and move his feet on the branch. His stomach is full, and his eyelids are heavy. He blinks twice and then goes into the dark hole to sleep.

Now the little woodcock knows that she must find a safer place for her baby chicks. She leaves the nest to search for a new home. In time she returns.

The sky is lighter now, and she must hurry before the fox and the weasel begin their morning hunt.

She clasps one of her tiny chicks between her legs, close against her body.

Carefully, very carefully, she rises into the air, carrying the chick.

She flies close to the ground, circling the edge of the woods. She dips under a branch and sees a sudden movement on her left. Quickly, she twists her body sideways.

The fox springs!

Feathers fly!

By only a few inches his sharp teeth miss their mark.

The brave little woodcock flies on, holding tightly to her baby chick.

She alights close to a patch of wood violets. Nearby is a leafy fern, and she leads the small chick in among its fronds. The dry and withered fern fronds make a sheltering curtain all around them. It is a perfect hiding place for her babies.

She flies away and before long returns with a second chick.

She makes two more trips. At last her family is safe.

A weasel passes by, but he does not see the family hiding under the fern.

As the woodcock gathers her babies under her warm feathers, she hears the last sleepy call of the whippoorwill.

Whip-poor-will . . .

The first rosy glow of sunlight spreads softly through the woods, awakening the creatures of the day.

The violets lift their purple and white blossoms to the warm light as the little woodcock tucks her head under her wing and goes to sleep.